The Incredible Bible Stories
Volume 3

Piyatina

Profile

The Incredible Bible Stories – Volume 3 is a captivating collection of biblical narratives showcasing a diverse array of stories: Rahab's courageous act of hiding Israelite spies in Jericho, the miraculous crossing of the Jordan River, the dramatic fall of Jericho, Achan's sin leading to Israel's initial defeat at Ai, the cunning deception by the Gibeonites to secure a peace treaty, Joshua's poignant farewell, the prophetess Deborah's triumphant leadership, and Gideon's heroic feats including saving Israel from the Midianites with a small but valiant army, as well as his relentless pursuit and defeat of the Midianite kings, Zeba and Zalmunna.

Each tale embodies themes of faith, obedience, and divine intervention, offering profound lessons for all readers. Volume 3 invites readers to explore these timeless lessons through inspiring stories and memorable characters.

Piyatina, MBA

Dedication

This book is lovingly dedicated to my father, the late S. P. Anthony Cruze, a valiant wounded veteran of the Indian Army. His sacrifices and valour were the beacon that inspired me to chase my dreams and stand firm against adversity. He was the architect of my perseverance and the champion of hard work.

In equal measure, I dedicate this work to my mother, the late Mary Stella Cruze, a steadfast pillar of support alongside my father and my guiding star. Their unwavering faith and boundless love for me have been the wind beneath my wings, propelling me to embrace my passion.

To my parents, to whom I owe my all, this book stands as a tribute—a testament to the seeds of knowledge they sowed in my heart and the dreams they nurtured, allowing me to turn them into reality.

Acknowledgements

My deepest gratitude is extended to the Almighty for the knowledge and inspiration bestowed upon me in the writing of this book. His guidance has been indispensable.

I wish to convey my heartfelt thanks to my husband, Dr G. Rajendran, and my son, R. Jasper Sheleph, for their unwavering support and assistance throughout this journey. Special thanks are due to Pastor T. Durairaj for his invaluable supervision.

Lastly, my appreciation goes out to the readers of 'The Incredible Bible Stories, Volume 3.' Your time and support are deeply valued. It is my sincere hope that this book will not only inspire and educate but also captivate your imagination.

The Incredible Bible Stories
Volume 3

Contents

From Joshua chapter 1 to Judges chapter 8

1. RAHAB AND THE SPIES

After the death of Moses, the Lord's faithful servant, the Lord spoke directly to Joshua, son of Nun and Moses' trusted assistant: 'Moses has passed away, and now it is your time to lead the Israelites across the Jordan River—the very land I promised to them. Every place where your foot treads (set foot) shall become your inheritance.

From the wild expanses (stretch) of Lebanon to the flowing Euphrates River, encompassing the territory of the Hittites and stretching toward the western sea, the land is yours. No adversary will prevail against you throughout your days, for I am with you, just as I was with Moses. I will neither fail you nor abandon you. Your task now is to divide this inherited land among the people.'

'Be strong and exceedingly courageous. Obey all the instructions that Moses gave you. Do not deviate from them, either to the right or to the left, so that you may prosper wherever you go. Continually study this book of the law, meditate on it day and night, and faithfully follow all that is written in it.

By doing so, you will achieve success. Do not be afraid or discouraged, for the Lord your God is with you.'

Joshua, the leader of Israel, issued a command to the officers: 'Instruct the people to prepare provisions—food fit for human consumption. In three days, you will cross the Jordan River and take possession of the land that the Lord God has promised.'

Joshua then addressed the Reubenites, Gadites, and half the tribe of Manasseh: 'Remember the words spoken by Moses. The Lord God has granted you rest and this land. Your wives, children, and livestock will remain on this side of the Jordan. However, all the valiant and courageous men must lead the other tribes across the river, fully armed, and assist their brothers until the Lord grants them rest and establishes their inheritance. Afterward, you will return to your allotted land, which Moses assigned to you.'

And their response? A pledge etched in faith: 'We'll follow your lead and go wherever you send us. Just as we obeyed Moses, we will obey you. May the Lord God be with you, as He was with Moses. Be strong and courageous.'

Later, Joshua dispatched two spies to gather intelligence about the land of Jericho. They arrived at the house of Rahab and took refuge there. However, word reached the king of Jericho: 'Some Israelites have come here tonight to spy on our land.'

Consequently, the king sent men to Rahab's house to apprehend the intruders. But Rahab concealed the two Israelite men. When questioned by the men of Jericho, she replied, 'They came, but I am unaware of their origin. They departed under cover of darkness before the gates were closed. Their whereabouts remain unknown. If you act swiftly, you may catch up with them.' But Rahab led the two Israelites to the roof, and she hid them among bundles of flax (a plant used to make linen).

The king's men pursued the spies to the Jordan River, to the shallow fords (stream). As soon as the king's men departed, the city gates were sealed.

Rahab approached the spies before they retired for the night and declared, 'I recognize that the Lord has granted you this land, and we all tremble in fear of you. The entire population is weakened by dread. We have heard of the Lord's miraculous parting of the Red Sea for you and the defeat of the Amorite kings, Sihon and Og. Our hearts melted upon hearing these accounts. For the Lord your God reigns supreme in heaven above and on earth below. In return for my kindness to you, swear by God's name that you will also extend kindness to my father, mother, brothers, sisters, and all their possessions, and spare our lives from destruction.'

The men replied, 'We pledge our lives as a guarantee for your safety if you do not betray us. When the Lord grants us this land, we will honour our promise and show kindness to you.' Rahab then lowered them from the window using a rope, as her house was built into the town wall.

She instructed the men, 'Seek refuge in the mountains and remain hidden there for three days until the search party gives up. Once they return, you can proceed safely.'

Before departing, the Israelites made an agreement with Rahab: 'When we conquer this land, tie a scarlet cord in the window through which you lowered us. This will signify safety for you and your family—your father, mother, brothers, and sisters. However, anyone who leaves your house and ventures into the street will not be our responsibility. We will be blameless, but those within your home are under our protection. But if you betray us and reveal this matter, then we will be released from the oath you made us swear.'

Rahab agreed, saying, 'May it be as you have spoken.' She sent the men away and secured the scarlet cord in the window. The men of Israel abode in the mountain for three days until the pursuers returned. Despite thorough searching along the way, the pursuers were unable to locate the Israelites.

Later, the two Israelites descended from the mountain, crossed the river, and approached Joshua. They recounted all that had transpired and declared, 'Truly, the Lord has delivered the land into our hands. Indeed, all the people of the country are faint-hearted because of us.'

Early the next morning, Joshua and all the Israelites set out from Shittim and camped near the Jordan River.

2. CROSSING JORDAN RIVER

After three days, the officers went through the camp giving instructions to the people: 'When you see the Levites priests carrying the Ark of the Covenant of the Lord, move from your position and follow them. Maintain a distance of two thousand cubits (approximately

45.72 centimetres per cubit) and do not approach it. This way, you will know the path, as you have not traveled this way before.'

Joshua addressed the people, saying, 'Sanctify yourselves, for God will perform wonders among you tomorrow.' He then instructed the priests, 'Take the Ark of the Covenant and lead the way before the people.' The priests obeyed, carrying the Ark as they walked ahead.

The Lord spoke to Joshua, declaring, 'Today, I will exalt you in the eyes of all Israel. They will recognize that I am with you, just as I was with Moses. Command the priests carrying the Ark of the Covenant to stand firm in the Jordan River when they reach the edge of the river.'

'Now choose twelve men from the tribes of Israel—one from each tribe.'

'Command them to take twelve stones from the midst of the Jordan River, where the priests stood, and carry those stones with them. Leave the stones at the place where you will camp tonight. Then command them to pass before the Ark of the Lord into the middle of the Jordan.'

Joshua gathered the Israelites and proclaimed, 'Listen to the words of the Lord your God. You will know that the living God is among you, and He will drive out the Canaanites, Hittites, Hivites, Perizzites, Girgashites, Amorites, and Jebusites before you. The Ark of the Covenant, representing all the earth, will pass ahead of you into the Jordan. As soon as the priests' feet touch the waters of the Jordan, the flow from above will cease, and the waters will stand as a heap.'

So, the people left their camps to cross the Jordan River. And the priests, bearing the Ark of the Covenant, went before the people. It was the harvest season, and the Jordan River was overflowing its banks.

Joshua gathered the twelve chosen men from each tribe and instructed them the words of the Lord. 'Pass before the Ark of the Lord into the middle of the Jordan. Each of you should take a stone upon your shoulder, corresponding to the number of tribes in Israel.' The men followed Joshua's command. They took the twelve stones and carried them to the place where they set up their camp. Joshua then placed those twelve stones in the middle of the Jordan, at the spot where the priests' feet had stood.

As soon as the feet of the priests carrying the Ark touched the brim (outer margin) of the water, the water that descended from above toward the salt sea stood still and rose in a heap. They backed up a great distance to a town called Adam, beside Zaretan.

The priests, who carried the Ark, stood in the middle of the river until Joshua conveyed all the commandments of Moses and executed all the commands of the Lord. The priests stood firmly on dry ground while all the people crossed the Jordan River. After everyone had completely crossed over, the priests also passed over with the Ark in the presence of the people.

The children of Reuben, Gad, and half the tribe of Manasseh, fully armed, crossed over ahead of the rest of the Israelites. Approximately forty thousand (40,000) people were prepared for battle on the plains of Jericho. On that day, the Lord magnified Joshua in the eyes of all Israel, and they revered (respected) him just as they had revered Moses throughout his lifetime.

The Lord spoke to Joshua, saying, 'Command the priests who bear the Ark to come up out of the Jordan.' Joshua promptly instructed the priests to ascend from the river. As soon as the priests stepped out of the midst of the Jordan with the Ark of the Covenant of the Lord and set their feet on the riverbank, the waters of the Jordan returned to their place and flowed as they had before.

After emerging from the Jordan River on the tenth day of the first month, the people set up camp on the east border of Jericho. They named this place Gilgal, signifying that the Lord had removed the disgrace associated with their time in Egypt. Joshua took the twelve stones they had retrieved from the Jordan and erected them in Gilgal.

Joshua addressed the Israelites: 'In the future, when your children inquire about the meaning of these stones, tell them that the Israelites crossed the Jordan on dry ground, just as the Lord had done at the Red Sea. The waters parted, allowing us to pass. This remarkable event will be known throughout the earth, and people will revere the Lord your God forever.'

After hearing all that the Lord had accomplished for the Israelites, the hearts of the Amorite and Canaanite kings melted, and their spirlts were drained of enthusiasm and energy.

The children of Israel wandered in the wilderness for forty years, during which time all the men of war perished because they failed to obey the voice of the Lord. The Lord swore that they would not see the promised land flowing with milk and honey.

3. THE FALL OF JERICHO

Later, the Israelites camped in Gilgal. On the fourteenth day, they observed the Passover feast in the evening on the plains of Jericho. The following day, they consumed unleavened bread (without yeast or raising agent) and roasted corn from the land. From that day onward, the manna ceased to fall, and that year they ate the produce of Canaan.

And when Joshua was near Jericho, he looked up and saw a man standing before him, with a sword in his hand. Joshua approached the man and asked, 'Are you on our side or our enemies'?' The man replied, 'Neither. I am the captain of the Lord's host.' Overwhelmed, Joshua fell to the ground, worshipped, and enquired, 'What message does my Lord have for his servant?' The captain of the Lord's host instructed Joshua, 'Remove your shoes, for the ground where you stand is holy.' Joshua promptly complied.

Jericho was tightly shut up because of the presence of the children of Israel. No one went out or came in. The Lord spoke to Joshua, saying, 'I have given you Jericho, its king, and its mighty warriors.'

Joshua relayed the Lord's instructions: 'All the men of war shall march around the city once a day for six days. Behind them seven priests shall walk, each carrying a ram's horn trumpet and blowing it. Followed by them will be the priests carrying the Ark of the Lord. On the seventh day, the priests shall go around the city seven times, and they shall blow a long blast with their trumpets. And when you hear the sound of a prolonged blast from the trumpets, all the people shall shout as loud as they can. Then the city walls will collapse, and you shall enter. But until that appointed day, refrain from shouting or making any noise.'

Joshusa woke up early the next morning. The priests carried the Ark of the Lord. Seven priests, each holding a ram's horn trumpet, walked ahead of the Ark of the Lord. They walked blowing the trumpets continually. A set of armed men marched in front of the priests blowing the trumpets. Another set of armed men followed the priests carrying the Ark of the Lord. On the second day also, they circled the city once, and then returned to camp. They repeated this process daily for six days.

On the seventh day, at dawn, the Israelites circled the city of Jericho seven times, following the same pattern. As the priests blew a long blast on their trumpets during the seventh round, Joshua addressed the people: 'Shout! The Lord has given you the city.' However, he issued a solemn warning: everything within Jericho was to be utterly cursed—devoted to destruction.

Despite this, Rahab and her household received mercy because she had sheltered the Israelite spies. Joshua emphasized that anyone who kept forbidden items would bring a curse and trouble upon the entire Israelite camp. Yet, the gold, silver, and vessels made of brass and iron were to be dedicated to the Lord's treasury.

The people erupted in a mighty shout as they heard the priests blowing their trumpets. The city walls crumbled and fell flat, allowing the Israelites to enter and conquer the city. They spared nothing—men, women, young and old, cattle, sheep, and goats—all met the same fate.

Meanwhile, Joshua instructed the two men who had scouted the land: 'Go to Rahab's house and bring her out, along with everything she possesses, just as you promised.' The young men obeyed, rescuing Rahab, her parents, brothers, sisters, and all her relatives. They ensured Rahab's and her family's safety outside the Israelite camp. Rahab continued to live among the Israelites until the end.

The Israelites set the city ablaze, sparing only the gold, silver, and vessels made of brass and iron. Those valuable items were placed in the treasury of the Lord's house. And Joshua invoked this curse: 'May the curse of the Lord fall on anyone who tries to rebuild the town of Jericho. Anyone who builds Jericho will lose his firstborn while laying the foundation and his youngest son while he sets up the gates.'

Thus, the Lord stood by Joshua, and news of his remarkable deeds spread throughout the land.

4. ACHAN'S SIN AND FALL OF AI

The Israelites transgressed (violated) by taking forbidden items, and Achan from the tribe of Judah committed trespass by seizing some of these accursed things. As a result, the children of Israel provoked the Lord's anger.

Joshua then dispatched men from Jericho to spy on the city of Ai. Upon their return, they advised Joshua, 'Send two or three thousand men to capture Ai; let not all our people struggle there, as it is sparsely (thinly) populated.' Acting on this advice, approximately three thousand men were sent. However, during the battle, the Israelites fled before the men of Ai, resulting in the deaths of thirty-six Israelite soldiers. Joshua and the elders expressed their grief by tearing their clothes, falling face down to the ground, and throwing dust on their heads before the Ark of the Lord until evening.

Joshua lamented, filled with anguish. O Lord God, 'Why have You led these people across the Jordan, only to deliver them into the hands of the Amorites? We would have been content to remain on the other side of the river. But now, Lord, the Israelites have turned their backs before their enemies. The Canaanites and all other nations will surround us, erasing our name from the earth. What will become of the honour of Your great name?'

In reply, the Lord addressed Joshua, 'Why do you lie prostrate (lying flat) on your face? Stand up! The children of Israel have sinned and violated my covenant. They have taken the accursed (cursed) things and hidden them among their belongings. Consequently, they could not stand before their enemies, but turned their backs. Destroy the accursed thing, or my presence will no longer be with you.'

Stand up, Joshua, the Lord said. 'Here are the words of the Lord, the God of Israel: Convey to the Israelites: "Purify yourselves tomorrow, for the Lord has identified an accursed thing among you. You will never defeat your enemies until you remove those things from among you."'

'Tomorrow, present yourselves by tribes, and the Lord will reveal the guilty tribe. From that tribe, the Lord will select the guilty family, and each member will come forward. The one who took the accursed thing will be burned with fire, along with all that belongs to him, because he violated the Lord's covenant and committed a disgraceful act in Israel.'

The next morning, Joshua rose early and gathered the Israelites by their tribes. The tribe of Judah was chosen, and from that tribe, Achan was singled out. Joshua addressed Achan, saying, 'My son, give glory to the Lord God of Israel. Confess to the Lord and tell me what you have done; do not hide anything.'

Achan replied, 'I have indeed sinned against the Lord. I coveted (desired possession) a beautiful Babylonian robe, along with silver and gold. And I buried them in the ground within my tent with the silver hidden underneath.'

So, Joshua sent messengers, who hurried to Achan's tent and retrieved the forbidden items. They brought Achan, along with the silver, garments, gold, his sons, daughters, oxen, donkeys, sheep, and his tent, before Joshua and all the children of Israel. They stood in the presence of the Lord. Then they took them to a valley. Joshua then addressed Achan, saying, 'Why have you brought this trouble upon us? The Lord will trouble you this day.' Subsequently, all Israel stoned Achan and burnt them with fire. They piled a great heap of stones over him, naming it the valley of Achor. Then the Lord's fierce anger abated.

The Lord spoke to Joshua, encouraging: 'Do not fear or be discouraged. Go to Ai with all your fighting men. I have given you the king of Ai, his city, and his land. You will do to Ai, and it's king, as you did to Jericho. However, this time you may keep the spoils and livestock after the city's destruction.'

Joshua selected thirty thousand mighty warriors and sent them out by night. He instructed the people, 'Wait behind the city, not venturing too far, but be prepared for action. As I approach the city with the people, the men of Ai will come against us, and we will flee before them. They will pursue us until we draw them away from the city. For they will say, "The Israelites are running away from us as they did before." Then, while we are luring (attracting) them away, you will rise up from your ambush (act of concealing oneself) positions and take possession of the city. The Lord your God will deliver it into your hands.

When you capture the city, set it on fire. These are my orders; do what the Lord has commanded.'

The next day, Joshua rose early in the morning and went with the elders of Israel to Ai, before the people. The entire force that was with him marched and approached the city, camping on the north side of Ai. There was a valley between them and Ai. Joshua selected about five thousand men and positioned them in ambush between Bethel and Ai, on the west side of the city. After setting up the people for the night on the north and west side of the city, Joshua stayed in the midst of the valley.

When the king of Ai noticed the Israelites, he and all his people hurried out early in the morning to engage in battle at an appointed time before the plain. He was unaware of the people hiding in the ambush behind the city.

Then Joshua and all Israel pretended to flee toward the wilderness, as if they were defeated. All the people of Ai were called together to pursue Joshua and the Israelites, drawing them away from the city. No one remained in Ai or Bethel who did not join the pursuit. The city was left unguarded as they followed Israel.

The Lord instructed Joshua, saying, 'Stretch out the spear that is in your hand toward Ai.' Joshua obeyed, extending the spear in his hand toward the city. As soon as he did so, the people lying in ambush arose, ran, and swiftly entered the city, setting it ablaze.

The men of Ai looked back and saw the smoke rising from the city to the sky, with no escape route. The Israelites who fled to the wilderness turned back against their pursuers. Seeing the rising smoke and taking over of the city by the people hidden in ambush, Joshua and the Israelites turned and attacked the men of Ai. Not a single person survived or escaped.

The Israelites struck down twelve thousand (12,000) men and women of Ai that day. Joshua did not withdraw his outstretched hand until the inhabitants of Ai were defeated. He burnt Ai and made it a heap forever.

The king of Ai was brought to Joshua alive. He then hanged the king of Ai on a tree until evening. At sunset, the Israelites took down the king's body, threw it at the entrance of the city gate, and piled a great heap of stones over it.

In obedience to the Lord's command, Joshua and the Israelites spared only the livestock and the spoils as plunder. Upon Mount Ebal, Joshua erected an altar made of whole stones. On these stones, he meticulously inscribed the law of Moses in the presence of the entire assembly: elders, officers, judges, strangers, and the Levite priests who bore the ark of the covenant. With unwavering diligence, Joshua read aloud every word of the law, including the blessings and curses recorded in the book. Not a single word was omitted from what Moses had commanded.

5. GIBEONITES DECEIVE ISRAEL

Upon learning of Joshua's successful conquests in Jericho and Ai, the people of Gibeon resorted to cunning tactics disguised as ambassadors to Joshua. They took old sacks upon their donkeys, old wine bottles, wore old clouted shoes (patched) upon their feet, and wore old garments. Even their provision included dry and mouldy (rotten) bread. Then they approached the camp at Gilgal, met Joshua and the men of Israel, and claimed that they came from a faraway country to secure an association with Israel.

But the men of Israel said to the Hivites, 'Perhaps you live among us, and how can we make a treaty with you?' They told Joshua, 'We are your servants.' Joshua asked them, 'Who are you and where are you from?' They replied, 'We have come from a distant country.'

'We heard the fame of the Lord God and all that He did in Egypt. We have also heard what He did to the two kings of the Amorites, King Sihon of Heshbon and King Og of Bashan. Our elders and all the people of our country instructed us to take victuals (food supplies) for the journey and to meet you and say,

"We are your servants; make a league with us. The bread was hot when we departed from our houses, but now it's dry and mouldy. The wine in the bottles was new when we filled them, and our garments and shoes have all become old due to the long journey.'"

The men of Israel took their victuals without seeking guidance from the Lord. Joshua then established peace and league with them, and allowing them to live. The assembly's leaders agreed to this arrangement with a binding oath.

At the end of three days, after making a league, the Israelites heard that they were their neighbours, and they dwelt among them. So the children of Israel journeyed and went to their cities of Gibeon, Chephirah, Beeroth, and Kirjathjearim on the third day. But the Israelites did not attack them because the Israelite leaders had sworn to them in the name of the Lord, allowing them to live.

Then the people of Israel grumbled against their leaders. But the leaders said to the assembly, We cannot touch them. Let the wrath (great anger) be upon us because of the oath we swore to them. Let them be wood cutters and water carriers for the entire community.

Then Joshua called the Gibeonites and said, 'Why have you deceived us by saying we are from a faraway country when you dwell among us? Now therefore, you are cursed and will be slaves who cut wood and carry water for the house of my God.'

They answered that they were so afraid of their lives, 'because the Lord thy God had commanded Moses to give you all the land and destroy all the inhabitants of the land. Behold, we are in your hands; do what seems good and right for you to us.' And Joshua saved the Gibeonites from the hands of the Israelites, and they did not kill them.

Adonizedek, the king of Jerusalem, heard about Joshua and how the inhabitants of Gibeon made peace with Israel. They feared Gibeon because it was a great city—one of the royal cities—where all the men were mighty. So Adonizedek, the king of Jerusalem, joined hands with the other kings of the Amorites: King Hoham of Hebron, King Piram of Jarmuth, King Japhia of Lachish, and King Debir of Eglon. Their purpose was to attack Gibeon, as Gibeon had already made peace with Joshua and the children of Israel. Therefore, the five kings of the Amorites gathered together, camped before Gibeon, and waged war against them.

The men of Gibeon, realizing their peril, sent messengers to Joshua in Gilgal, pleading, 'Come and save us from all the Amorite kings dwelling in the mountain.'

Joshua, with unwavering determination, travelled all night, leading his mighty men of valour from Gilgal. The Lord said, 'Fear not, for I have given you victory over them. Not a single one of them will be able to stand before you.' They caught the Amorites by surprise, and the Lord intervened, defeating their plans and chasing them. As the Amorites fled down toward Bethhoron, the Lord hurled great stones from heaven upon them, and they perished. More of the enemy died from hail than by the swords of the Israelites.

On the day the Lord granted victory to the Israelites over the Amorites, Joshua said in front of Israel: 'Sun, stand still upon Gibeon, and Moon, linger in the valley of Ajalon.' Miraculously, the sun remained suspended in the sky, refusing to set a whole day, and the moon stayed until the Israelites had vanquished (defeated) their enemies. Never before or since has the Lord responded so directly to the voice of a man; indeed, the Lord fought for Israel.

During the battle, the five kings fled and hid in a cave at Makkedah. Aware of this, Joshua instructed the men of Israel to roll large stones and place them at the entrance of the cave and to post guards. Since the Lord had delivered the enemies into the hands of the Israelites, none dared speak a word against Israel.

After a fierce battle, the five kings were captured and hung upon trees until evening. During sun set, Joshua ordered their bodies to be cast into the cave they were hiding, which was then sealed with large stones. The Lord granted victory to the Israelites, enabling them to conquer the cities of Makkedah, Libnah, Lachish, Eglon, Hebron, and Debir. In a remarkable campaign, Joshua extended his dominion from Goshen to Gibeon, encompassing the entire region from Kadeshbarnea to Gaza.

6. JOSHUA'S FAREWELL

Joshua, the leader of the Israelites after Moses, engaged in prolonged warfare against various kings and cities. No city sought peace with the Israelites except the inhabitants of Gibeon. The Lord hardened their hearts to wage war against Israel, fulfilling His command to destroy them completely, a directive originally given to Moses.

Joshua meticulously distributed the land to the twelve tribes of Israel, adhering faithfully, just as the Lord had commanded Moses. Finally, after years of struggle, the land found rest from war. Joshua and the children of Israel emerged victorious, defeating a total of thirty-one kings and securing their possession of the Promised Land.

The Lord said to Joshua, 'You are growing old, and there is still much land left to possess. Therefore, divide this remaining land as an inheritance among the nine tribes and the half tribe of Manasseh. However, for the tribe of Levi, Moses did not allocate any land, because the Lord God Himself was their inheritance.'

One day the children of Judah approached Joshua. Caleb, son of Jephunneh, said to Joshua, 'I was forty years old when Moses, the man of God, sent me to explore the land of Canaan from Kadeshbarnea. I returned and gave an honest report, but my brothers who accompanied me discouraged the people from entering the Promised Land. Despite this, I remained steadfast and followed the Lord my God wholeheartedly.'

'On that day, Moses made me a promise: the land where your foot has trodden shall be granted to you and your descendants forever because of your unwavering devotion to the Lord. Despite my eighty-five years, I remain as strong as when Moses first sent me to explore the land of Canaan. My vigour endures—I can still travel and fight as I did before. Therefore, I request the mountain that the Lord spoke of on that day.'

Joshua blessed Caleb, son of Jephunneh, and allotted Hebron to him as his portion of land. Previously, Hebron was known as Kirjath-arba, named after Arba, a renowned hero among the descendants of Anak.

The inheritance of Simeon was within the inheritance of the children of Judah; for the part of Judah was too much for them. Moses did not allocate any inheritance to the tribe of Levi, as their role was to serve as priests of the Lord, and the Lord God was their inheritance. Instead, they were provided with towns to live in, along with pasturelands (land for grazing animals) for their livestock and property for their substance. All the cities that the Levites possessed were forty-eight with their suburbs.

After the land was divided among the other tribes, the Israelites did give Joshua an inheritance in Timnathserah, as he had requested. All the good things the Lord had spoken to the house of Israel were fulfilled.

Joshua summoned the tribes of Reuben, Gad, and the half-tribe of Manasseh. He commended them, saying, 'You have faithfully followed all of Moses' commands and have also obeyed my instructions. Throughout this time, you have not deserted your fellow Israelites and have been loyal to obey the commands of the Lord.'

'Now that the other tribes have found rest in their allotted lands, you return to the homes that the Lord has given you as your possession. Love the Lord your God, serve Him wholeheartedly, and diligently keep the commandments and laws that Moses imparted to you.' Joshua then blessed them and sent them on their way, and they returned to their tents. The Lord granted Israel rest from their enemies for a prolonged period.

Meanwhile, Joshua himself grew old. He assembled all the elders, leaders, judges, and officers of Israel and addressed them: 'I am now advanced in years. As promised by the Lord your God, I have apportioned (allotted) the nations as an inheritance for your tribes. Therefore, be exceedingly courageous and unwavering in your commitment to follow the path outlined in the book of the Law of Moses. Do not deviate to the right or left. Avoid any association with the remaining nations among you. Refrain from invoking (calling upon) the names of their gods, serving them, or swearing by them. Instead, hold fast to the Lord, your God, just as you have done until this day. The Lord has already driven out powerful and mighty nations before you; no one has been able to withstand you.'

'Indeed, a single Israelite shall pursue a thousand enemies, for the Lord fights on your behalf, fulfilling His promise. Be vigilant and love the Lord, your God, with all your heart. If you revert to the remnants of these nations, they will ensnare you, become traps, and afflict you like scourges (whips) in your sides and thorns in your eyes. Their influence will harm you until you are driven from this good land that the Lord has bestowed upon you.' Joshua assembled all the tribes of Israel—the elders, leaders, judges, and officers—and they presented themselves before God.

Joshua, as a leader, conveyed the divine message to the entire assembly of Israelites.

> In ancient times, your father lived beyond the river. I personally guided Abraham throughout the entire land of Canaan, multiplying his descendants and granting him Isaac. To Isaac, I bestowed both Esau and Jacob. Mount Seir became Esau's inheritance, while Jacob and his children journeyed to Egypt.
> I sent Moses and Aaron, inflicting plagues upon Egypt, and subsequently led you out. As you reached the Red Sea, the Egyptians pursued you with chariots and horsemen. Yet, the Red Sea engulfed

(submerged) them, and your own eyes witnessed this miraculous event.

- ➢ I led you into the land of the Amorites, where they waged war against you. However, I intervened and defeated them, allowing you to inherit their territory.
- ➢ Balak desired Balaam to pronounce a curse upon Israel, but I did not heed that request. Consequently, Balaam ended up blessing you instead.
- ➢ You crossed the Jordan River to reach Jericho, and I granted you victory over the Amorites, Perizzites, Canaanites, Hittites, Girgashites, Hivites, and Jebusites.
- ➢ I have bestowed upon you land that you did not cultivate, cities that you did not construct. The vineyards and olive groves are yours, even though you did not plant them.
- ➢ Therefore, fear the Lord and serve Him sincerely with a true heart. The

people responded, 'We will serve the Lord, for He brought us out of the land of Egypt, out of the house of bondage.'

Joshua warned them, 'The Lord God is both holy and jealous. If you forsake the Lord, He will not forgive your rebellion and sins. Instead, disaster will befall you, and destruction awaits.' Nevertheless, the people firmly declared, 'No, we will serve the Lord and obey His voice.'

Joshua inscribed these words in the book of the Law of God and placed a large stone beneath an oak tree (known for bearing acorn fruit and having a lifespan of up to a hundred years). This stone served as a witness near the holy place of the Lord. Afterward, Joshua sent the people to their allotted homelands.

After all these events, Joshua, the son of Nun and a devoted servant of the Lord, passed away at the age of one hundred and ten years. He was laid to rest in his allotted inheritance in Timnathserah, situated on Mount Ephraim. Throughout Joshua's lifetime and even during the days of the elders who outlived him, the Israelites remained faithful in their service to the Lord.

The children of Israel also fulfilled an important task: they buried the bones of Joseph, which they had brought with them from Egypt. This burial took place in the land of Shechem—a parcel of land that Jacob had acquired for one hundred silver coins. Additionally, Eleazar, the son of Aaron, passed away, and he was buried on Mount Ephraim, a place that pertained to Phinehas, his son.

7. PROPHET DEBORAH

Following Joshua's death, the Israelites sought guidance from the Lord: 'Who shall lead us in battle against the Canaanites?' The Lord's response was clear: 'Judah shall go.' Judah then rallied his brother, saying, 'Join us in this fight, and we will support you in return.' Consequently, Simeon joined forces with Judah. Through divine intervention, the Canaanites and Perizzites fell before them, resulting in the defeat of ten thousand men.

However, when the children of Israel turned to other gods and provoked the Lord, He allowed their enemies to prevail over them. The Lord then raised up judges to deliver the people from their adversaries. Sadly, after the judges passed away, the Israelites reverted to worshipping other gods, surpassing even the sins of their forefathers. The Lord declared, 'I will no longer drive out the nations that Joshua left unconquered upon his death. Instead, I will test Israel to determine whether they will remain faithful to the Lord, as their ancestors did.' These unconquered nations included the five rulers of the Philistines, the Canaanites, the Sidonians, and the Hivites residing in Mount Lebanon.

The Lord's anger burned against Israel, leading Him to deliver them into the hands of Chushanrishathaim, the king of Mesopotamia. For eight years, the children of Israel served under this foreign dominion. However, when the Israelites cried out to the Lord, He raised up a deliverer named Othniel—son of Kenaz and Caleb's younger brother. The Spirit of the Lord came upon Othniel, empowering him to serve as a judge for Israel. Othniel led the people into battle, and the Lord granted victory over Chushanrishathaim. As a result, there was peace in the land for forty years. Eventually, Othniel, the son of Kenaz, passed away.

When the children of Israel once again committed evil in the sight of the Lord, He raised up Ehud—a left-handed Benjamite—as their deliverer from the king of Moab after eighteen years of oppression (cruelty). Ehud's cunning actions resulted in the death of about ten thousand valiant men. As a consequence, the land enjoyed peace for eighty years.

After Ehud's demise, the children of Israel came under the dominion of Jabin, the king of Canaan. Sisera, as the commander of Jabin's army, wielded (possessed) a formidable force of nine hundred iron chariots. For two decades, he oppressed the Israelites severely.

During this period, Deborah, the wife of Lapidoth, served as a prophetess who spoke by divine inspiration and judged Israel. She dwelt beneath a palm tree in a location known as Deborah, situated between Ramah and Bethel on Mount Ephraim. The Israelites sought her wisdom to resolve their disputes.

One day, Deborah summoned Barak, the son of Abinoam, and conveyed the Lord's command: 'Go to Mount Tabor with ten thousand men from Naphtali and Zebulun, and I will deliver Jabin and his army into your hands.' Barak responded, 'If you go with me, I will go; if not, I will not go.' Deborah assured him, 'I will certainly accompany you, but understand that the glory of this victory will not be yours—it will be the Lord's doing, as He will deliver Sisera into the hands of a woman.' And so, Deborah went with Barak to Kedesh.

Barak called upon Zebulun and Naphtali, leading ten thousand men with Deborah by his side. Meanwhile,

Heber—a descendant of Jethro (Moses' father-in-law)—had distanced himself from the Kenites and set up his tent near Kedesh. Heber then relayed to Sisera that Barak had ascended Mount Tabor. In response, Sisera mobilized all nine hundred of his iron chariots and his entire army, advancing toward the Kishon River.

Deborah said to Barak, 'Go, for the Lord has delivered Sisera into your hands; the Lord is marching before you.' Barak led his chariots and ten thousand men down the slopes of Mount Tabor. When Barak attacked, the Lord threw Sisera, his chariots, and his army into panic. Sisera abandoned his chariot and fled on foot. Barak pursued the chariots and defeated them, leaving no survivors.

After fleeing on foot, Sisera sought refuge in the tent of Jael, the wife of

Heber the Kenite. Peace between King Jabin of Hazor and Heber's family facilitated this encounter. Jael welcomed Sisera, saying, 'Come into my tent, my lord; have no fear.' Sisera entered, and she covered him with a blanket. Thirsty, Sisera asked Jael for water. Instead, she gave him milk to drink and covered him once more. Sisera instructed her, 'Stand at the tent door, and if anyone enquires whether anyone is here, say, 'No.'

While Sisera slept from exhaustion, Jael quietly approached him with a hammer and a tent peg (nail). She drove the peg through his temple, securing it to the ground, causing his death.

As Barak pursued Sisera, Jael went out to meet him and said, 'Come, I will show you the man you are seeking.' Barak entered the tent and discovered Sisera dead, the tent peg piercing his temple. On that day, Israel recognized that God had defeated Jabin, the king of Canaan, and Israel grew stronger until they completely vanquished him.

Then Deborah and Barak, the son of Abinoam, sang a song:

"Praise the Lord! I will sing praise to the Lord God of Israel.

When You marched from the field of Edom, the earth trembled, the heavens poured, and the mountains melted.

Few people remained in the villages of Israel until I, Deborah, the mother of Israel, arose.

When Israel turned to new gods, war erupted at the gates; was a shield or spear seen among the forty thousand.

My heart is with the rulers of Israel who volunteered themselves among the people. Praise the Lord.

Wake up, wake up, Deborah, wake up! Sing a song. Barak, rise and lead your captives.

The Lord made me have domain over the mighty.

The princes of Issachar were with Deborah. As Issachar, Barak was also sent into the valley.

Among the divisions of Reuben, there was significant indecision. Gilead remained beyond the Jordan. Why did the tribes of Dan stay in the ships? Asher remained along the coast, seeking refuge in breaches (gaps or opening made in the wall).

Zebulun and Naphtali risked their lives in the battlefield. The kings of Canaan fought near the waters of Megiddo, but they did not seize any treasures.

The stars from heaven fought against Sisera.

The Kishon River swept them away. O my soul, you have trodden the mighty.

The horse hooves pounded the mighty.

Meroz be cursed bitterly, said the angel of the Lord. 'For they did not help the Lord against the mighty.'

Jael the wife of Heber, the most blessed among women.

Sisera asked for water, and she gave him milk and butter in a lordly bowl. Her hand reached for the tent peg and pierced his temples. He sank and fell at her feet, bowed, and died.

Sisera's mother looked out of the window and wondered, 'Why is his chariot delayed?' She kept saying to herself, 'They must be dividing the spoils among every man and woman.

Thus, let all Your enemies perish, O Lord! But let those who love you, shine like the sun in its strength."

And so, there was peace in the land for forty years.

8. GIDEON THE SAVIOUR

The Lord delivered the children of Israel into the hands of the Midianites for seven years due to their renewed disobedience. Unable to endure the cruelty of the Midianites and Amalekites, the Israelites sought refuge in dens and caves in the mountains to hide.

Whenever the Israelites planted their crops, the Midianites, Amalekites, and the people of the east would launch attacks against Israel. The invaders descended like a swarm of locusts with their livestock and camped on the land, devastating the crops. Israel was left without tents or sustenance—neither for themselves nor for their livestock. The Israelites were greatly impoverished (weakened). In distress, the Israelites cried out to the Lord.

In response to their cries, the Lord sent a prophet with a stern message: 'I told you that I am the Lord your God; do not worship the gods of the Amorites, in whose land you now live. Yet, despite this warning, the Israelites persisted in disobedience.'

Later, under an oak tree in Ophrah, the Angel of the Lord appeared to Joash's son, Gideon. Gideon, secretly threshing wheat (separating the grain from the straw) in a winepress to evade the Midianites, received an unexpected declaration: 'The Lord is with you, you mighty man of valor.' However, burdened by their suffering, Gideon questioned, 'Oh my Lord, why does this adversity persist? If the Lord is truly with us, why have we been delivered into the hands of the Midianites?'

Then the Lord turned to him and spoke: 'Go with the strength you have, and you will save Israel from the Midianites; I am sending you.' Gideon replied, 'But Lord, how can I rescue Israel? My clan is the weakest in the whole tribe of Manasseh, and I am the youngest in my entire family.' The Lord assured him, 'I will be with you, and surely you will defeat the Midianites as if you are fighting against a single man.

Gideon, seeking confirmation from the Lord, said, 'If I have found grace in your sight, show me a sign to prove that you have spoken to me. Wait here until I bring my present and set it before you.' And the Lord replied, 'I will stay here until you return.'

Gideon earnestly went inside and prepared a meal—a young goat and unleavened bread. He arranged the meat in a basket and the broth in a pot, then carried it to the angel of the Lord under the oak tree and presented it. The divine instruction came: 'Take the meat and bread, place them upon the rock, and pour the broth.' And Gideon, obedient, followed the command.

Then the angel of the Lord touched the meat and unleavened bread with the tip of the staff (a long wooden stick) that was in his hand. Fire flared up from the rock, consuming the meat and bread. Afterward, the angel of the Lord disappeared from Gideon's sight.

When Gideon realized that he had encountered the angel of the Lord, he exclaimed, 'Alas, O Lord God! I have seen the angel of the Lord face to face.' But the Lord reassured Gideon, saying, 'Peace be unto you; do not fear. You will not die.'

And Gideon built an altar there and named it Jehovahshalom, which is in Ophrah to this day. That same night the Lord said to Gideon, 'Take the second bull from your father's herd, the one that is seven years old. Pull down the altar of Baal that your father owns and cut down the grove beside it. Then build an altar on this hilltop and take the second bull and offer a burnt sacrifice on the wood of the grove which you shall cut down.'

So, Gideon took ten of his servants and did as the Lord had commanded. He did it at night rather than in the daytime because he was afraid of his father's family and the people of the town.

Early the next morning, the men of the city discovered that the altar of Baal was demolished and the grove cut down and lay beside it. They inquired among themselves, attributing (blaming) the act to Gideon, the son of Joash. The people demanded that Joash bring his son Gideon forward, for he deserved to die because he had broken Baal's altar. Joash responded to the crowd, 'Why are you defending Baal? Are you trying to save him? Whoever fights for him shall be put to death by morning! If Baal is truly God, let him defend himself and destroy the one who broke down his altar.' And from that point on, Gideon was known as Jerubbaal.

Now all the Midianites, the Amalekites, and the eastern people joined forces, crossed the River Jordan, and camped in the valley of Jezreel. Then the Spirit of the Lord came upon Gideon, and when he blew a trumpet, the men of Abiezer followed him. Gideon sent messengers to summon all the men of war from the tribes of Manasseh, Asher, Zebulun, and Naphtali, and they came up to meet him.

Gideon said to the Lord, 'If You will save Israel by my hand, as You have promised, then prove it to me. I will place a fleece of wool on the floor. If the fleece is wet with dew and the ground is dry, then I will know that You will rescue Israel by my hand.' The next day, that is exactly what happened. When he rose early in the morning and squeezed the fleece, he collected a bowlful of water.

Then Gideon said to the Lord, 'Do not be angry with me; let me make one more request and test one more time with the fleece. This time, let the fleece remain dry, but let there be dew on the ground around it.' So that night, God did as Gideon asked. Only the fleece was dry, whereas the ground was covered with dew.

9. GIDEON DEFEATS MIDIAN

Then Jerubbaal (also known as Gideon) and his assembled forces rose early and encamped near the well of Harod, positioning themselves to confront the

Midianites in the valley of Moreh. It was at this juncture that the Lord addressed Gideon: "You have too many people. Therefore, announce to the army: Anyone who is fearful and afraid may turn and depart from Mount Gilead." As a result, twenty-two thousand (22,000) individuals chose to return home, leaving ten thousand (10,000) steadfast warriors.

However, the Lord persisted in His instructions to Gideon: 'Even now, the numbers remain excessive. Bring the troops to the water, where I will discern (distinguish) who will accompany you and who will not.' Gideon dutifully complied, leading them to the water's edge.

The Lord said to Gideon, 'Separate those who lap the water with their tongues like a dog from those who kneel down to drink.' Three hundred (300) of them drank from cupped hands, lapping like dogs. The rest of them got down on their knees to drink. And the Lord said to Gideon, 'With the three hundred (300) men that lapped the water, I will rescue you and deliver the Midianites in your hands. Let all the others go home.' So, Gideon sent the rest of the Israelites home and kept the three hundred (300) men.

They took provisions and their trumpets in their hands. The Midianite camp lay in the valley just below Gideon's position.

On that very night, the Lord spoke to him: 'Rise and descend to the Midianite host, for I have already delivered it into your hands. However, if fear grips you, take your servant Phurah and venture to the Midianite camp. Listen carefully to what the people say. After that, your hands will be strengthened.' Gideon and Phurah descended to the outskirts of the camp, where the armed men lay. The Midianites, the Amalekites, and all the children of the East lay in the valley, as numerous as grasshoppers. Their camels, too numerous to tally, stretched beyond the horizon like the sands along the seashore.

As Gideon arrived, he overheard a man narrating a dream to his companion: 'I saw a loaf of barley bread tumble into the midst of the Midianite camp. Striking a tent with tremendous force, the tent overturned and collapsed.' The companion promptly interpreted the dream: 'This can only signify the sword of Gideon, son of Joash—the Israelite. God has already delivered Midian and their entire host into his hands.' Upon hearing this prophetic revelation,

Gideon humbly bowed and worshipped the Lord.

Gideon returned to the camp of Israel and declared, 'Arise, for the Lord has delivered the Midianites into your hands.'

He divided the three hundred men into three groups, equipping each with a trumpet and an empty pitcher (pot) containing a lamp. Gideon instructed them: 'Observe my actions closely. When I reach the edge of the camp, follow suit. As I and my companions blow the trumpets, you too shall sound the trumpets on every side of the camp, proclaiming, "The sword of the Lord and the sword of Gideon."'

In the middle of the night, just past midnight, and during a shift change among the guards, Gideon and the hundred men accompanying him approached the camp's edge. There, they simultaneously blew their trumpets and shattered the pitchers they held. All three groups followed suit. They blew their trumpets and shattered the pitchers. With lamps in their left hands and trumpets in their right, they raised their voices in unison: 'The sword of the Lord and the sword of Gideon.'

Every man stood in his designated place around the camp. As the three hundred Israelites blew their trumpets, the Lord caused every man in the camp to fight against each other with their swords, and all the Midianites fled, crying out. The Midianites fled to Bethshittah. Meanwhile, the Israelites seized control of the waters of Jordan. Additionally, they captured Oreb and Zeeb, the two princes of the Midianites, and dealt them a fatal blow.

10.KINGS ZEBAH AND ZALMUNNA

The men of Ephraim expressed their displeasure because Gideon had not called upon them to join the battle against the Midianites. Their frustration escalated into a heated argument with Gideon. In response, Gideon said, 'What have I accomplished compared to you?'

He posed a thought-provoking question: 'Are not the gleanings from Ephraim's harvest—those leftover grapes—more valuable than the entire yield of the Abiezer clan?'

Despite their exhaustion, Gideon and the three hundred (300) men crossed the Jordan River, pursuing their fleeing enemy. Upon reaching Succoth, Gideon approached the towns people with a plea: 'Please provide food for my weary followers. We are in pursuit of Zebah and Zalmunna, the kings of Midian.'

The princes of Succoth retorted, 'Do you already have Zebah and Zalmunna in your custody, that we should provide food for your army?' Gideon's reply was unyielding: 'Once the Lord delivers Zebah and Zalmunna into my hands, I will punish you with the thorns of the desert.' Similarly, the men of Penuel echoed the sentiments of their counterparts in Succoth. Gideon issued a solemn declaration: 'Upon my safe return, I shall dismantle this tower.'

Zebah and Zalmunna led an army of fifteen thousand (15,000) men. On that fateful day, one hundred and twenty thousand (120,000) soldiers lost their lives. Faced with this devastating defeat, Zebah and Zalmunna fled, but Gideon pursued them relentlessly (unforgiving) and ultimately captured their entire army.

Gideon returned from battle before sunrise. He declared to the men of Succoth, 'Here are Zebah and Zalmunna, about whom you ridiculed me, questioning, "Are Zebah and Zalmunna already in your hands, that we should give food to your exhausted men?"'

Gideon took the elders of the town and decided to teach a memorable lesson. He punished them with desert thorns. Additionally, he demolished the tower of Penuel and killed the men of the city. Gideon asked Zebah and Zalmunna, 'What kind of men did you kill at Tabor?' They answered, 'Like you. They had the look of a king's son.' Gideon replied, 'They were my brothers, the sons of my own mother. As the Lord lives, I would not kill you if you had spared their lives.'

Gideon said to Jether his firstborn, 'Attack them.' But he did not do so, because he was afraid and he was still a youth. Then Zebah and Zalmunna pleaded with Gideon, 'Kill us yourself.' So, Gideon executed Zebah and Zalmunna and seized the ornaments from their camels' necks.

The Israelites said to Gideon, 'You, your son, and your grandson should rule over us for you have rescued us from Midian.' However, Gideon responded, 'I will not rule over you, nor will my son. The Lord will be your ruler.' Despite this, Gideon had a request: he asked each person to give him the earrings they had taken as plunder from their fallen enemies. The Ishmaelite enemies wore gold earrings.

The Israelites agreed, saying, 'We will gladly give them.' They spread out a garment, and each one threw the gold earrings taken from the plunder. The combined weight of the gold earrings was one thousand seven hundred shekels (one shekel being approximately 11 grams). Additionally, they contributed royal ornaments, pendants, purple garments worn by the kings of Midian, and the chains from their camels' necks. Gideon then fashioned the gold into an ephod, a priestly apron, and placed it in Ophrah, his city. Little did he know that this ephod would become a trap for him and his family.

Thus, Israel triumphed over Midian, and the Midianites never regained their strength. The land enjoyed forty years of peace during Gideon's leadership. Jerubbaal returned home and settled down. He had seventy sons, all of whom were his descendants. Additionally, he had a son named Abimelech, born to him through a strange woman. As Gideon reached old age, he passed away. He was laid to rest in the tomb of his father, Joash, in Ophrah of the Abiezrites.

However, as soon as Gideon breathed his last, the Israelites turned away from the Lord. They abandoned their faith and began to worship Baalim, making Baalberith their god. In their forgetfulness, they neglected the Lord—the very God who had rescued them from the clutches of their enemies. Furthermore, they failed to honor the legacy of Jerubbaal, despite all the remarkable deeds he had performed for Israel.

Thank you for being a part of this incredible journey, and I look forward to sharing volume 4 with you very soon.